Farm Animals

Illustrated by Sylvaine Peyrols
Created by Gallimard Jeunesse and Sylvaine Peyrols

MY FIRST DISCOVERY PAPERBACKS

Who lives in the farmyard?

Chickens, ducks, geese, guinea fowl, turkeys...

There are many different breeds of chicken.

Chickens live on farms
all around the world.

Cock

Hen

The cock
and hen mate.

The hen sits on her
eggs to hatch them.

Three weeks
later, the chicks
are born.

The mother hen shows her chicks
how to pick up grain
with their beaks.

Ducks take off and land clumsily. They waddle when they walk.

Ducks spend most of
their time on or near
water. Their webbed
feet help them swim.

Drake

Duck

Ducklings will lose their yellow down and grow new feathers.

They dive down to look for
plants and worms.

Geese live in flocks.

Gander

Goose

When a
goose is upset,
it hisses.

Before mating, the gander dances round the goose.

When her goslings hatch,
the goose leads them to the water.

She shows them plants
that are good to eat.

You can't
miss the turkey
among the other
farmyard birds!

Guinea fowl make a lot of noise!

Only pigeons fly well on the farmyard.

A turkey cock ruffles up his feathers to attract a mate.

How many different farm animals
can you see in this picture?

They spend a lot of time
eating grass.

Sheep give us meat, milk and wool.

The males are
called rams,
the females
are ewes, the
babies are lambs.

In spring, the sheep are sheared for their wool.

They live in a flock
and eat grass all day.

Cattle (bulls and cows) eat grass.

Female cattle
are called cows,
the babies are calves.

Bulls are male cattle.
They can be fierce.

Bullocks are kept
for meat.

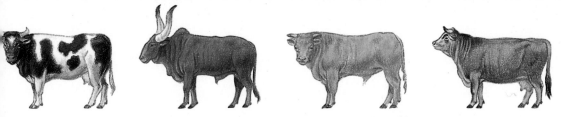

Some cattle have huge horns, some hardly any.

A cow produces milk
when she has a calf.

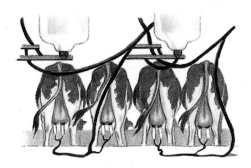

Cows are milked
by machines.

Rabbits don't walk; they hop.

Rabbits
are kept in a fenced
area of grass, or in a hutch.

A buck rabbit dances for his doe.
He thumps the ground with his back legs.

Baby rabbits are pink, bald and blind when they are born.

Pigs have good hearing and
a keen sense of smell.

They use their
snouts to find
the roots and nuts
they love to eat.

Piglets have curly tails.

There are many different kinds of pigs.

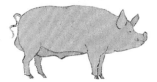

The boar is
the male.

The sow is
the female.

The piglet is
the baby.

A sow can feed
up to fourteen piglets.

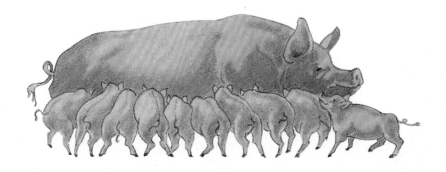

Each morning, the cock crows
and wakes up the animals
on the farm.

The farmers get up early to feed
and look after all the animals.

MY FIRST DISCOVERY PAPERBACKS

Classics

Dinosaurs
The Egg
Farm Animals
Firefighting
Flowers

Fruit
Homes
The Jungle
Planes
The Seashore

The Town
Trains
Trees
Vegetables
Water

Torchlights

Animals Underground
Arcimboldo's Portraits
Insects
Inside the Body
Life below the City

Translated by Sarah Matthews
ISBN: 978-1-85103-755-1
© Éditions Gallimard Jeunesse, 2008.
English Text © Moonlight Publishing Ltd, 2022.
English audio rights Ⓟ Moonlight Publishing Ltd, 2022.
First published in the United Kingdom in 2022
by Moonlight Publishing Ltd,
2 Michael's Court, Hanney Road
Southmoor, Oxfordshire, OX13 5HR
United Kingdom
Printed in China

MOONLIGHT
PUBLISHING